# HORSE TRANSPORT
## IN LONDON

# HORSE TRANSPORT
## IN LONDON

SAMANTHA RATCLIFFE

TEMPUS

For my husband Mark Porter. Thank you for your love and support.

*Frontispiece*: Illustration of a horse bus in Queen Victoria Street, *c.*1890.

First published 2005

Tempus Publishing Limited
The Mill, Brimscombe Port,
Stroud, Gloucestershire, GL5 2QG
www.tempus-publishing.com

© Samantha Ratcliffe, 2005

British Library Cataloguing in Publication Data.
A catalogue record for this book is available from the British Library.

ISBN 0 7524 3458 6

Typesetting and origination by Tempus Publishing Limited.
Printed in Great Britain.

# Contents

# Introduction

It is hard today to imagine London without a bus or a taxi. They are recognisable icons of the city but before the 1820s they simply did not exist. The wealthy, of course, had horses and private horse-drawn carriages, but the only way for most people to get around the city was on foot. The London of the seventeenth and eighteenth centuries was predominantly a walking city. As London expanded, the demand for an easier means to get around the city grew. The first organised transport workers were the watermen, who hired their boats on the Thames. From the 1620s hackney coaches began to appear on the roads. These were available for private hire and soon became popular, mingling on London's streets with gentlemen's coaches. The term 'Hackney' comes not from the area of London as one might imagine, but is, in fact, a French import. The word *haquenee* refers to a slow, ambling horse. The proliferation of these vehicles was so great that regulations were introduced to limit their number and in 1694 the Hackney Coach Commissioners were set up to oversee the trade. The state of the roads was terrible. Despite the limitations on the number of hackney coaches, they were competing on London's narrow, poorly maintained thoroughfares with private carriages and short and long-haul stage coaches that ran out to London's surrounding villages. As early as 1800, road traffic congestion was a problem. Only a few streets in the centre of the city were paved, an area known as 'the stones'. In order to preserve the condition of these, hackney coaches were given the monopoly in using them. No other vehicles were allowed into the area.

  This selection of photographs and ephemera has been chosen from the collections of London's Transport Museum and deals with the vehicles that revolutionised transport in the Victorian and Edwardian eras. The first chapter looks at horse cabs, which first appeared in London in 1823. The cabriolet, or cab, first used in France, was much smaller and lighter than a hackney coach and was drawn by one horse rather than two. These new cabs soon became the vehicle of choice for the 'men about town'. They charged cheaper fares, had newer, more innovative vehicles and used better horses than the older, more cumbersome hackney carriages. The number of horse cabs increased over the years, until they replaced hackney coaches. The photographs seen here are mainly of the popular 'hansom cab' that dominated London's streets in the late nineteenth century, but other examples are included. The latest image is from the 1920s, which shows the persistence of these vehicles despite the fact that the motor engine had taken over most cabs.

The major innovation for public transport was the horse omnibus. Again imported from France, the first vehicle in London was introduced by George Shillibeer in July 1829. He had worked as a coachbuilder in Paris and had brought back the idea of a vehicle running over a set route, for a set fare. The term 'omnibus' (later shortened to 'bus') was a Latin term meaning 'for all' but the vehicles were very much a middle-class mode of transport. The price of a penny for the whole journey along the New Road, was still out of reach for London's poor. The first vehicles were prohibited from entering the paved central area of London, but in 1831 the hackney coach monopoly of 'the stones' came to an end and many rival companies and vehicles began to appear, eventually leading to streets bustling with buses, going to many different destinations. The chapter on buses is the largest in this book, reflecting the dominant impact they had on London's transport. Earlier images are in illustration form of the various designs of vehicles and the people who operated them. The photographs date from 1855 and show the evolution of vehicle design and development of companies from the earliest bus of the London General Omnibus Company, through to the last services operating in 1914. They mainly consist of the driver and conductor posing with a vehicle, but also included are views of the staff, horses and stables that were vital in keeping the service running. There was remarkably little attention paid to recording images of the horses at the time, as these were seen mainly as capital goods, the mere engines of the vehicles, an expensive commodity that cost a lot to keep and depreciated in value very quickly. When the petrol engine was developed the advantages to the bus companies was seen immediately – cheaper, cleaner, no feeding, bridling, shoeing, stabling or veterinary costs – and soon horses were replaced. The final images in the bus chapter show the sad end of the vehicles which had revolutionised travel in Victorian London.

The final chapter deals with the vehicle that revolutionised working-class travel, the horse tram. Imported this time from America rather than France, the vehicles ran along a steel rail embedded into the road. It was a lot easier for a horse to pull a vehicle along a rail than a poor road surface and as a result larger vehicles carrying more passengers could run for the same cost. Companies introduced cheap, workman's fares and a whole new market for public transport was born. Trams co-existed with the horse bus and were never seen as competition because of the difference in class of their respective passengers. The first vehicles introduced in 1861 were a failure but the idea was seen as a good one and soon a number of tram companies were formed. Again the images in this book are predominantly of driver and conductor posing proudly with their vehicle, but some tickets and staff shots are included. The later photographs again show the sad demise of the vehicle that was replaced, not by the petrol engine, but by electricity. Very early on when companies were being formed the disadvantages of the horse were known and the desire to run a cheaper, more efficient service meant that innovation was welcome. Electrification of lines began as early as 1901, but the horse-drawn vehicle remained in some areas until 1915 and often ran along the same routes with their electric counterparts. Eventually, of course, even electric trams left London's streets, the last running in 1952.

For one hundred years horse-drawn vehicles dominated London's streets. They had revolutionised the travelling experience and allowed an ever-expanding London to be traversed quickly and cheaply. Of course the noise, smell, and the environmental impact of thousands of horses on the city's streets should not be underestimated. The images in this publication reflect the heyday of these vehicles and hopefully show the elegance of changes in design and the social impact that the first public transport network had. The text accompanying these images can only provide an introduction to the subject of horse-drawn public transport in London in the period. I have found the following publications invaluable in putting together this book and would recommend them to anyone interested in learning more.

Day, John R., *The Story of the London Bus – London and Its Buses from the Horse Bus to the Present Day* (1973)
Day, John R., *London's Trams and Trolleybuses* (1977)
Lee, Charles E., *The Horse Bus as a Vehicle* (1974)
May, Trevor, *Gondolas and Growlers – The History of the London Horse Cab* (1995)
May, Trevor, *Victorian and Edwardian Horse Cabs* (1999)
Oakley, E.R., *The British Horse Tram Era* (1978)
Shadwell, Roy, *Horse Omnibus – Entertaining and Instructive Episodes from the History of its Horses* (1994)
Taylor, Sheila (ed.), *The Moving Metropolis – A History of London's Transport since 1800* (2001)
Thompson, John, *Horse-Drawn Omnibuses* (1986)
Wilson, Geoffrey, *London United Tramways – A History 1894-1933* (1971)

Copies of most prints reproduced in this publication may be purchased by writing to the address below and quoting the reference number in square brackets at the end of each caption. Personal visits to view the photographic collection, which covers all aspects of London's public transport, can be made by appointment.

Samantha Ratcliffe, Curator (Photographs & Ephemera)
Photographic Library
London's Transport Museum
Covent Garden
London
WC2E 7BB

# Acknowledgements

The following colleagues from London's Transport Museum have been invaluable with their comments and advice in putting together this publication: Graham Page, David Ruddom, Oliver Green, David Bownes, Hugh Robertson, Anna Rotondaro and Simon Murphy. Thank you for all your help.

one

# The Horse
# Cab
# 1820s-1920s

In the eighteenth century London was predominantly a walking city. The only alternative on the roads was the horse. For the wealthy this meant horse-drawn coaches, as can be seen in this detail from an engraving entitled 'Views of London No2', showing the entrance of St Georges Road, or the obelisk turnpike, with a view of the Royal Circus.

As London grew so did the demand for public transport. From the 1620s hackney coaches (from the French *haquenee*, used to describe a walking horse) started to appear on the roads, mingling in with the gentlemen's coaches. They were available for public hire and their numbers soon multiplied. The streets of London became overcrowded, as can be seen here in this satirical print by Waterman Rowlandson from the *Miseries of London* series, 1807, showing a street scene in which coach traffic blocks the way.

Stage coaches (like this model from the collection of London's Transport Museum) were available for long-distance journeys and from the 1820s short-stage coaches were put into service, which ran along short fixed routes around London. They were not available for private hire, so were more the forerunners of the omnibus, about which more shall be said later.

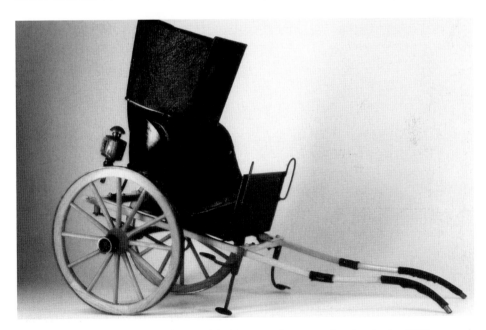

Horse cabs or 'cabriolets' were first used in France and came to London in the 1820s, around the same time as short-stage coaches. They were smaller and lighter than hackney coaches and were drawn by one horse rather than two. Various designs developed over the years. This model of a coffin cab is in the collection of London's Transport Museum. The name derived from the shape of the seat in which the passenger sat. The driver sat in an uncovered seat to the side of the passenger.

This illustration of a 'Coffin cab' outside the Old Bailey, by George Cruikshank, was published in Charles Dickens' *Sketches by Boz* in 1836.

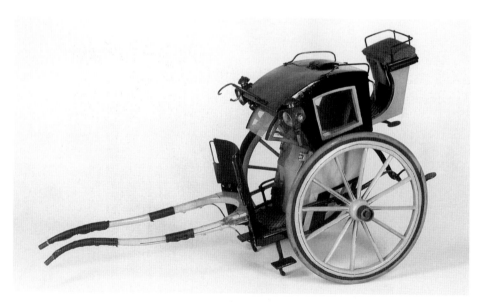

Joseph Hansom, after whom the hansom cab is named, took out a patent for his cab in 1834. His patent was modified many times, most notably by John Chapman. The 'Hansom cab' that proliferated on Victorian streets should have more correctly been termed the 'Chapman cab'. This model, from London's Transport Museum, shows the hansom cab in its final form as developed by coachbuilders Forder & Co. in 1873. The hansoms became known as the 'gondolas' of London.

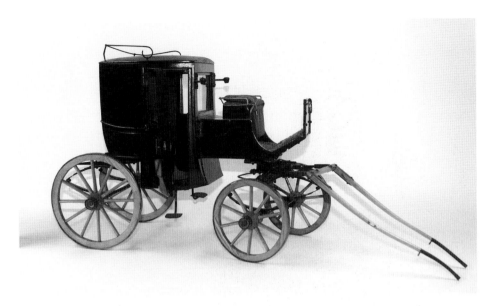

From about 1830, a four-wheel Clarence cab, known as a 'growler', appeared on London's streets alongside hansoms. A sturdier vehicle, these cabs could not compete with hansoms for style or comfort but tended to fare better for passengers with a lot of luggage, hence they could later often be found outside railway stations. This scale model of a 'growler' is in the collection of London's Transport Museum.

EXTERIOR OF CAB, WITH INDEX.

This 1860 engraving of a 'growler' cab features a design with an index to show the mileage of a journey. Fares in a cab were based on a standard charge per mile but passengers generally had to rely on the honesty of drivers to charge them the correct amount. The 'Patent Mile Index' was an early attempt to check the distance of a journey.

REYNOLDS'S IMPROVED PATENT SAFETY CAB.

New and improved designs for cabs appeared regularly in the press. This one from 1846 was Reynold's 'Improved Patent Safety Cab'. Many of the designs never actually made it onto the streets.

This illustration shows Harvey's 'Curricle Tribus', a large hansom cab designed to seat three people. It also carried a conductor to take fares and in this respect was similar to an omnibus. It was introduced by Mr Harvey of Lambeth House in 1847.

THE NEW PATENT CABRIOLET.

The 'Tribus' was said to have 'superior accommodation, safety and elegance' by the *Illustrated London News* when it published these illustrations of the vehicle in May 1847. Despite this assertion the public did not take to it. Very few were introduced and it soon disappeared.

THE NEW PATENT CABRIOLET.

The 'Tribus' had a rear entrance, similar to that on the omnibus, which made it easier for passengers to enter and exit.

The two-wheeled hansom was the most prominent of the horse cabs. In the early 1890s two thirds of London's cabs were hansoms and by 1897 they made up 69 per cent of total cabs on London's roads. This cab is in a London street in around 1898. [1998/20707]

One of the changes Chapman had introduced to Hansom's original patent was that the driver's seat was at the back behind the passenger. It would be hard to imagine it now in any other position. This image shows a passenger taking his seat around 1900. [2000/21427]

This hansom cab was operated by Thomas Tilling. He was a 'jobmaster', which meant he owned a number of horse-drawn vehicles for various purposes, including omnibuses and private carriages, as well as cabs. He also hired out horses to other companies including horse tram firms. He was the largest jobmaster in London and his company survived until the 1940s. This photograph was taken outside Greenwich station in 1897. [2004/3398]

This hansom is in the street outside Blackfriars station, c.1899. To the right, a boy is sweeping the road. Crossing sweepers were employed to clear the roads of dung and this was an essential job given the numbers of horses on London's roads. One thousand tons of dung were said to have been dropped on Victorian streets every day. This was gathered into huge dung heaps and sent off to market gardens around London to be used as fertiliser. [1998/72335]

This horse is drinking from a trough at Victoria Embankment. The Metropolitan Drinking Fountain and Trough Association, founded in 1859, provided a number of these watering stops, but many proprietors did not allow their horses to drink from them for fear of catching a waterborne disease. [1999/19190]

The horse of this empty hansom feeds from a nosebag. The cab is waiting in the Strand in 1916. The last horse cabs were still in use long after the First World War, despite the growth of the motor cabs, introduced to Britain's roads in the early 1900s. [1998/86875]

This hansom cab is in Piccadilly Circus, heading towards Eros with Regent Street leading away in the distance. Other horse-drawn vehicles can be seen, including an omnibus. [1998/85417]

A number of hansom cabs can be seen in the middle of the street in this image of the Strand, looking towards Fleet Street, *c*.1884. The photograph shows this section of the Strand as it appeared shortly after the removal of Temple Bar and the completion of the Royal Courts of Justice (the Law Courts), seen in the foreground to the left. [1998/44843]

The rear of a hansom cab can be seen following an omnibus in this view of Fleet Street, looking towards St Paul's Cathedral from a point just west of Shoe Lane. The road is crowded with horse-drawn vehicles and illustrates the fact that London's streets have always been congested. [1998/84120]

This view of Oxford Street, west of the Circus and looking east in June 1888, again shows horse cabs and omnibuses. It shows buildings that existed at the end of Argyle Street that have since been replaced by the Underground station. [1998/85483]

Here a hansom, and a 'growler' cab can be seen with other horse-drawn vehicles in the Strand looking east, with St Mary-le-Strand church in the distance. This is a scene from around 1890. [1998/44823]

The street here at Oxford Circus, c.1895, is full of hansom cabs. A boy is pulling a barrel organ in the foreground. [2004/6541]

This traffic scene in Queen Victoria Street in around 1900 shows a street full of hansom cabs as well as other horse-drawn vehicles. [2004/16837]

Here a line of horse-drawn cabs – hansoms and a 'growler' – standing in front of Ridler's Family Hotel, Holborn in 1897. [1998/23586]

The Strand in 1900 was always packed with horse-drawn vehicles. [2004/6538]

This view of Marylebone Road, with Madame Tussaud's on the left, shows a number of hansom cabs and other horse-drawn vehicles in 1895. [1998/44629]

This four-wheeled 'growler' cab is being loaded with parcels outside the London office of Kelly's Directories in the early 1920s. The centenary of the London cab was in 1923. At this time there were still 347 horse cabs on the streets, though these slowly dwindled until the streets were serviced exclusively by the motor cab. [2002/8803]

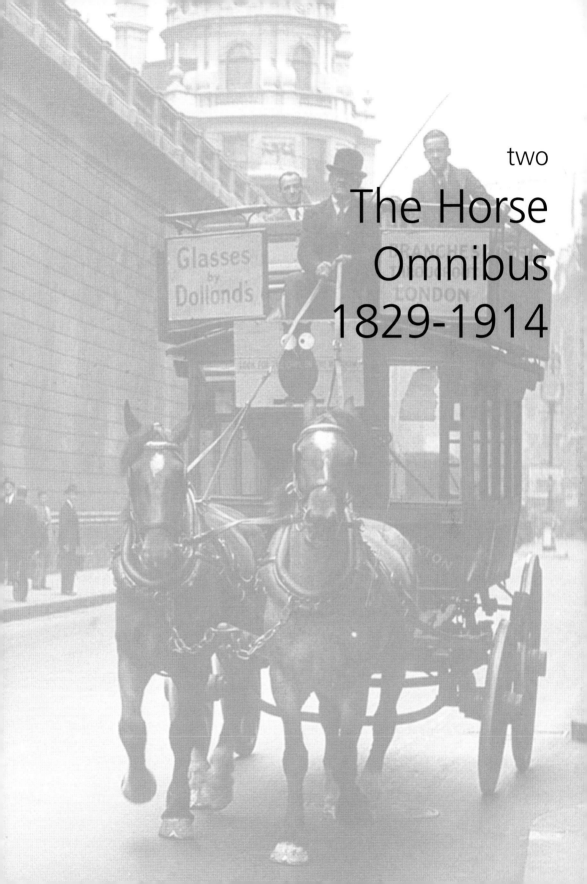

two

# The Horse
# Omnibus
# 1829-1914

As mentioned earlier, the forerunner of the omnibus was the short-stage coach, as featured in this illustration. Short stages carried pre-booked passengers at a fixed fare but they were slow and expensive. Ordinary people could not afford to travel on these vehicles.

The story of the London bus actually originates in France in 1662, when Blaire Pascal ran carriages over a fixed route. In Nantes, Stanislaus Baudry ran a service from a shop owned by a Mr Omnes. A sign above the door said 'Omnes Omnibus', a pun using the Latin term 'for all'. The term 'omnibus' stuck and was first used in Paris in 1828 when Baudry began running vehicles over ten routes. Over time 'omnibus' has been shortened to 'bus', the term we use today. This illustration shows a Paris omnibus in 1828.

The omnibus arrived in London in 1829 when George Shillibeer announced
that he was going to put into service two omnibus vehicles along the New
Road (now Marylebone, Euston and Pentonville roads). The vehicles would be
cheaper and more comfortable than short-stage coaches. The service began on
4 July. This advertisement appeared in *The British Traveller* in 1829.

George Shillibeer brought
the idea of the omnibus to
London from Paris, where he
had worked as a coachbuilder
for Jaques Lafitte, who ran a
service. The London service
was an instant success but
over the years Shillibeer
faced problems from growing
competition and eventually he
went bankrupt. He was sent to
debtor's prison but on release
changed his business into
'Shillibeer's Funeral Coaches',
and worked at this until the
end of his life. He died in
1866, aged 69. This portrait
was taken in his later life, in
around 1860. [1999/20254]

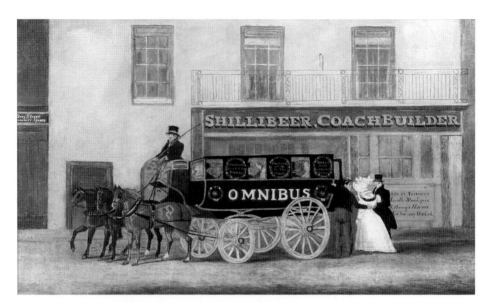

On returning from Paris in 1829, Shillibeer set up his coach-building and livery stables firm in Bury Street, Bloomsbury, with partner John Cavill. He began his omnibus service, which ran from Paddington to Bank along a five-mile route, which took about an hour. Shillibeer was banned from picking up passengers in central London – an area known as 'the stones' – because Hackney carriages had the monopoly there. This painting shows an omnibus and passenger at the Bury Street headquarters although the vehicle never actually ran from this site.

Shillibeer's service proved popular and within nine months he had 12 vehicles at work on the same route. During the 1830s new services sprang up, with rival bus operators competing for passengers, often racing each other to pick up fares. This was possible as the hackney coach monopoly of central London or 'the stones' was abolished in 1831. There were no fixed bus stops as we know them today. Passengers hailed a bus from the roadside. To stop the bus, passengers either banged on the roof or pulled on reins attached to the driver's arms! These methods were eventually replaced with bells. The elegant three-horse drawn vehicles began to be replaced with smaller two-horse vehicles as seen in this illustration.

*Opposite below:* Shillibeer's omnibus could carry up to 20 passengers and was drawn by three horses. He boasted it offered a safer and more comfortable ride than ordinary stagecoaches, as all passengers would ride inside. The vehicle was manned by a driver who sat up front, and a conductor who stood on a platform at the back entrance. He indicated to the driver when the vehicle should stop to pick up passengers and when to move on. The conductor also collected the fares. Although called 'Omnibus' (the Latin word meaning 'for all'), the fare of one shilling all the way was far beyond the means of the average worker in London, yet it was still less than the price of most short stagecoach rides. This replica of Shillibeer's original horse omnibus was built for the centenary celebrations in 1929 and is in the collection of London's Transport Museum. [1999/20129]

In order to distinguish himself from other companies using the term 'omnibus' on the side of their vehicles, Shillibeer elected to use his name instead. This can be seen in this cartoon, which appeared in a newspaper in 1831. The accompanying caption, parodying the use of the vehicles by a different class who could now afford transport, and the fact that the vehicles were considered respectable enough for women and children to travel in, read, 'Now then, Mounseer Shillibeer, I suppose you charges nothing for children – they takes up no room. There's only three on us, barring the little 'uns. Three tanners to Paddington, or no go!'. A tanner was sixpence, which was the fare from halfway along the route.

*Opposite, above-left:* This staged shot showing a woman revealing her ankles whilst getting on an omnibus possibly illustrates the contemporary concerns about women travelling on public vehicles. The passenger is obviously having difficulty with her large skirt. [2004/3392]

*Opposite, above-right:* Compare the image on the opposite page with this satirical print addressing the same issue of the suitability of omnibuses for women. In this image a woman passenger has got her crinoline caught in the entrance door, causing her to fall.

 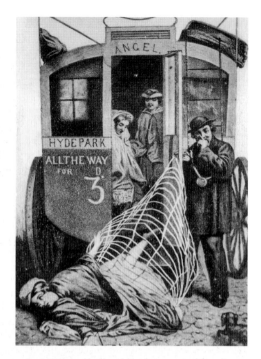

*Below:* Many new proposals for bus designs were put forward and ideas appeared in the press. This illustration shows Hunnybun & Vendens 'New Patent Safety Omnibus' of 1846. The accompanying publicity stated that the bus's low construction meant passengers could board without the aid of a step. This would make it more suitable for female passengers and their troublesome skirts.

This engraving, published in the *Illustrated London News* in 1860, shows De Tivoli's Patent Omnibus, which removed the nuisances usually associated with travelling on an omnibus (such as frequent trampling of toes and falling over one another's knees) by providing each passenger with a separate compartment. Each compartment faced the pavement and had a window in the side that could be lowered should the passenger wish to converse with the person in the next compartment. A bell in each section also allowed the passenger to communicate with the conductor. Note also the curtains in the vehicle's windows.

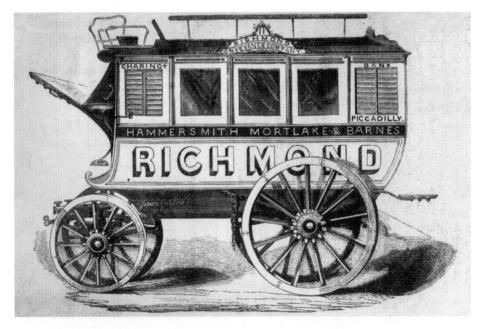

This engraving shows the Improved Omnibus (Narrow Gauge) built for the Richmond Conveyance Company. It had ventilation and a hole for a 'drop-light' in the roof.

One design innovation that did take off 1840s was the use of seats on the roof of the vehicle, seen here in this 1852 painting. Also in the 1840s large fleets of vehicles with different owners appeared. Certain companies dominated certain routes and one of the larger firms was owned by E. & J. Wilson, who ran their 'Favorite' line of buses from North London to the City.

THE NEW OMNIBUS.

This humorous idea for a new omnibus was featured in *Punch*, *c*.1870. It proposed buses should contain a barbershop, library, refreshment room and other facilities to make delays due to traffic congestion more comfortable for passengers.

Back-to-back seating along the centre of the roof became popular. These seats became known as the 'knifeboard', because of their similarity to the implement used for sharpening carving knives. This illustration from 1859 shows City clerks alighting from busy knifeboard buses at Bank at 9 a.m. in the 1870s.

*Opposite below:* This knifeboard bus from 1859 was one of the first of the London General Omnibus Company (LGOC). Its design is actually based on a number of entries into a competition the company held in 1856 to find an improved omnibus. The £100 prize was won by a Mr R.F. Miller, but the judges did not feel the design was good enough to build. This vehicle, then, ultimately comprised different elements of several designs. It ran on the Putney Bridge to London Bridge Railways route. [2004/10874]

THE PRIZE OMNIBUS OF THE LONDON GENERAL OMNIBUS COMPANY.

*Above:* Formed in 1855, the LGOC became the biggest firm in London up until the formation of London Transport in 1933. Actually formed in Paris, it began running horse bus services in London on 7th January 1856, and by the end of that year had become the largest operator in the capital. This illustration shows the company's 'Prize Omnibus'.

The only destination visible on this knifeboard bus is Westminster Bridge. The licence number is 7370. The Stage Carriages Act of 1832 made it compulsory for vehicles to be licensed. In 1838 drivers and conductors had to be licensed also. This photograph is from 1864. [1998/58076]

This knifeboard horse bus, licence number 6731, is owned by an independent operator. It calls at Bank, Holloway, Highbury, Islington and the City. It is loaded with gentlemen passengers in this picture from around 1865. [1999/20290]

This image, taken apparently in the same location, shows an LGOC knifeboard vehicle with the retained 'Favorite' livery of E. & J. Wilson's company. The vehicle has a 'decency board', a wooden barrier attached to the side of the roof to cover the view of ladies' ankles should they sit on the top deck. These were introduced in the mid–1860s and were also handy for advertisements. The vehicle does not appear to have brakes. They were not introduced until the 1890s. [1998/83643]

An iron rung ladder to reach the top deck can clearly be seen on this LGOC 'Favorite' 1860s knifeboard bus on service between Highbury, Bank, Holloway and London Bridge Railways. Note the prominent advertisement on the decency board. [1998/82882]

This bus for London Bridge Railways with 'Brompton' livery is loaded with passengers. It is a variation on the usual knifeboard bus in that some of the seats are facing toward each other. There are also curtains on the lower deck windows. [1998/20671]

This LGOC City Atlas bus was the first to cross Holborn Viaduct on
8 November 1869. It was driven by Thomas Grayson, thereafter known as
'Viaduct Tommy'. Holborn Viaduct was created to improve the approach
to the City of London from the west via the steep-sided Holborn Hill
and over the Fleet valley. The viaduct was built in the 1860s by the
Improvement Committee of the City of London and took six years and
over £2 million to complete – a huge cost for the time. [1998/83685]

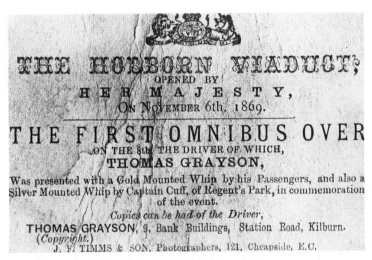

Many vehicles wanted to be the first across Holborn Viaduct and
congregated at 8 a.m. on the morning of the opening in a bid to win
the race. The barriers were removed and all the vehicles set off at speed.
Apparently Tommy 'cracked his whip, gave a flick to his spanking greys
and loosened the reins. He cut across a rival 'bus, blanketed a hansom
and steering into nearside rails... he made the pace'. To great cheers from
the crowd he was the first to cross the line and became famous along his
route. His passengers presented him with a gold-mounted whip to mark
his achievement. He also had large numbers of photographs and this
certificate printed to commemorate the event. [1998/57258]

One complaint against drivers was their racing at high speeds in a bid to get the most passengers. With no regulation and no official bus stops there was fierce competition for trade and for the pride of being the fastest vehicle. There were often races in the streets, sometimes with the encouragement of passengers. This illustration, taken from a Christmas card, shows rival buses at speed. The caption reads, 'Driver. 'Ere's a 'appy New Year an' no mistake'.

*Left:* Horse bus drivers and conductors were well-known characters on London streets and were often depicted in prints, satirical cartoons, newspaper articles and artworks. This idealised picture shows a smiling driver and jolly passengers. The cover across the driver's knees has the LGOC company name. Driving a bus was hard work as a working day consisted of 14 hours and there was no protection from the elements.

*Opposite below:* Conductors were also characters on London's streets. Here, rival omnibuses compete in 1837. The drivers are jeering at one another and the conductors are trying to persuade two female passengers to travel on their bus. Competition for passengers was fierce and conductors were not always seen as gentlemen in some of the methods they used to secure trade.

One well-known horse-bus driver was William Parragreen, known as 'Cast-Iron Billy'. He worked as a driver for forty-three years between 1834 and 1877. Billy started work with the London Conveyance Company but after 14 years' service the company was sold and he was made redundant. He next worked as a jobmaster, which was followed by two years' unemployment after which he secured a position with the London General Omnibus Company. He worked for the LGOC 14 hours a day, until his enforced retirement. Billy eventually lost his position as driver as he could no longer cope with competition from younger drivers. They were quicker to get along the routes and pick up passengers. Billy, as an old man, also needed help to get up onto the bus, and to hold onto the reins as he had partially lost the use of his left hand. Billy said, 'I can't sit at 'ome, my perch up there was more 'ome to me than anythink. Havin' lost that I'm no good to nobody; a fish out o' water I be'. Billy is pictured here with his conductor and bus in 1877. [1999/6540]

THE RIVAL OMNIBUSES.

## THE CONDUCTOR.

By me they goes it now into the city.

DANTE TRAVESTIED.

This illustration from around 1840 shows a horse bus conductor wrapped up against the elements. He is wearing a license badge. Drivers and conductors working within ten miles of the General Post Office were required to be licensed and wear numbered badges. To regulate these, a Registrar of Metropolitan Public Carriages was appointed by the Home Secretary.

This lithograph from around 1845 also shows a conductor plying for trade. He seems to be depicted more favourably than the previous image.

Here a driver and conductor are seen forcing a passenger onto the back of a bus in an attempt not to lose the fare. Printed across the door is the number of people the vehicle is licensed to carry. After the 1838 Act, it was compulsory to have this, as well as the words 'Metropolitan Stage Carriage' and the Stamp Office number clearly visible on every vehicle.

"ALL RIGHT."

This illustration appeared in *The Pictorial Times* in 1845 and shows a conductor clearly unperturbed that a passenger is falling from the back of his vehicle.

"Roy'l-Oak Roy'l-Oak
Archir Street."

These two watercolours
depict horse bus conductors
bound for Royal Oak, Archer
Street and Brixton Hill. They
were painted by Leonardo
Cattermole between 1850 and
1880.

"Brixton'ill Brixton'ill."

This image from a wood engraving dated 19 December 1863 shows a street scene with numerous passengers waiting in the rain with umbrellas. Many are attempting to board the already full bus. The engraving accompanied an article on the crowded and somewhat uncomfortable conditions on board a packed horse bus on a rainy night.

It was not only drivers and conductors that received press attention. The inconveniences of travelling by bus also raised comment. In this engraving the state of the roads is clearly an issue for travellers trying to get on the bus. The squalor of London streets can clearly be seen, a situation not improved by the horse dung, which was then trampled by horses' hooves. Crossing sweepers can be seen attempting to clear up some of the mess.

The cover of this edition of the *Illustrated London News*, dated 11 June 1859, depicts the crowded interior of a London bus. The image is based on *Omnibus Life in London*, an oil painting by W.M. Egley (a painting now held by Tate Britain), and some disgruntled faces can be seen.

*Overleaf:* The journeys on buses were immortalised in song. These two song sheets have the words and music for popular songs of the day; 'The Fun and Fuss of an Omnibus' included the lines, 'Come tumble in – there's room we bawl; Inside they cry "No room at all"; Here's the fat man enough for two; Oh let me out what shall I do?' 'The Miseries of an Omnibus' seems a somewhat bleaker look at a journey.

# THE FUN AND FUSS OF AN OMNIBUS,

## a new Comic Song

WRITTEN BY

# JOHN MAJOR,

Sung with unbounded applause by

# MR. FITZWILLIAM,

ALSO BY

*Mr. Morgan, Mr. Bruton, Mr. Howell, Mr. Glindon,*
*Mr. King, Mr. W. Rogers, Mr. G. Herbert,*

&c. &c.

ARRANGED WITH AN ACCOMPANIMENT FOR THE

# Piano Forte,

BY

# J. MONRO.

Ent. Sta. Hall.

M & N. Hanhart lith. Printers, 84 Charlotte St. Rathbone Place.

Pr. 2/-

# THE MISERIES OF AN OMNIBUS.

*Lithog.d & Printed by G.E. Madeley, Wellington S.t*

A COMIC SONG, SUNG BY

*Mr Fitzwilliam, Mr W. H. Williams & Mr Howell,*

*at Public Dinners, Concerts, &c.*

𝔚ritten by

J. E. CARPENTER,

*and respectfully dedicated to*

𝔗he 𝔄pollo 𝔊riffin 𝔊lee 𝔖ociety,

The Music Arranged by

S. GÖDBÈ.

*Ent. Sta. Hall.*                                          *Price 2/.*

LONDON.

Published by T. E. PURDAY, 50. St Pauls Church Yard,
SUCCESSOR (in this branch of the business) to COLLARD & COLLARD, late CLEMENTI & Co.
*Where the following Comic Songs are also published*

| | | | |
|---|---|---|---|
| THE COMET | 2/. | ALLOWED TO BE DRUNK ON THE PREMISES | 2/. |
| MY SON TOM | 2/. | GOING OUT A SHOOTING | 2/. |
| MISERIES OF AN OMNIBUS | 2/. | ST PATRICK WAS A GENTLEMAN | 1/6 |
| THE UNFORTUNATE MAN | 2/. | THE ONE HORSE SHAY | 1/6 |

Despite the satirical comment and complaints regarding journeys, vehicles, conductors and drivers, the London omnibus was there to stay and they dominated London's streets for many years. Here two LGOC knifeboard buses can be seen outside the White Lion Hotel, Putney Bridge, in around 1881. [1998/20636]

This view of Putney High Street in 1882 shows two buses. The front one numbered 762 runs via South Kensington Museum, Knightsbridge and Charing Cross. The rear bus runs via Fulham and South Kensington Museum. [1998/87202]

This one-horse LGOC vehicle from the 1880s has no seating on the roof. It was known as the 'Penny Bumper' because the fare was only 1d and it ran between Highbury Hill and Highbury station. These cheaper buses were introduced in periods of economic depression. Room could still be found for an advertising board to publicise Bryant and May matches. [1998/58085]

This one-horse single-deck bus with 'Saloon Bar' livery was known as the 'Ha'penny Bumper'. It was on service between Putney and Richmond. In place of a conductor the fares were dropped into a box overseen by the driver. [1999/6255]

In 1881 the London Road Car Company (LRCC) introduced this 'improved' knifeboard horse bus. It had easier access to the top deck by means of the staircase at the front and very small front wheels. The design was soon abandoned because of the danger of passengers falling from the staircase and being crushed by the rear wheels. [2002/8845]

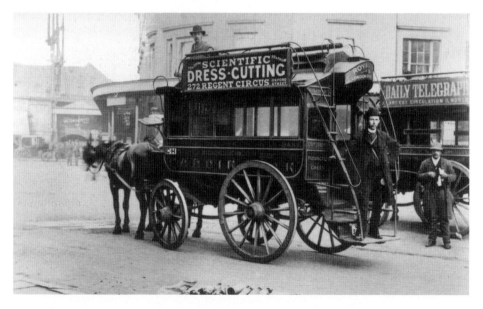

This LGOC bus shows twin iron rung ladders giving access to the upper deck either side of the conductor's platform. The bus stands in the forecourt of London Bridge station in 1887 on service between the station and Paddington Green via Oxford Street. [1998/83688]

This knifeboard bus stands outside the Albion Public House in Lauriston Road, Hackney in around 1885. Many bus routes began and terminated outside pubs. [1998/58080]

This photograph of a 'Favorite' knifeboard bus with driver and passengers has been retouched in places. The location is unknown. It appears to have a short working slip board saying 'Bank Only' covering the normal route details. [1998/58087]

This LGOC bus ran from the Bird in Hand pub on Hampstead High Street to town. It is seen being pulled by three horses, which were necessary in areas with steep hills. The image dates from around 1900. [2004/5249]

Here another three-horse bus is on service between Hampstead and Oxford Street. The bus has stopped at the foot of Rosslyn Hill. The third horse, known as the 'cock horse', was only hitched onto the vehicle at the foot of the hills. A boy was employed to wait at certain a spot for the bus to arrive. He would then attach the horse and when the bus got to the top he would unhitch and ride the horse back down again, ready for the next service. [1999/14775]

This LGOC knifeboard bus is outside the Eyre Arms public house, in St Johns Wood in 1890. A brake on the rear wheel can clearly be seen. These were first introduced in the late 1870s and consisted of a shoe applied to the rim of the wheel by a lever pressed by the driver at the side of his seat. [1998/84503]

Another addition to bus design of this period was the adoption of a curved staircase at the rear of the bus instead of a platform and iron rung ladder. This addition, along with the use of decency boards, made it much easier for women to ride on the top deck with dignity. Three women can be seen on this photograph taken outside The Horns public house at Kennington in around 1895. The route codes on the front of the vehicle, KP & KC, denote the route between Kennington Park and Kensington Church. The U sign is the stable code. [1998/84643]

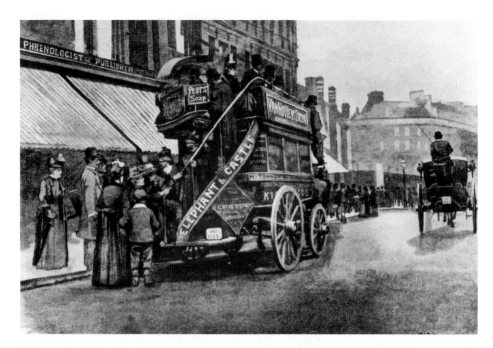

The rear, curved staircase can be seen more clearly in these three images. This illustration, taken from the 1891 edition of *London City*, features a knifeboard bus in New Bridge Street.

This shot of the rear of a bus with curved staircase, taken *c.*1900, clearly shows the proliferation of advertising used on horse buses. First introduced in the late 1840s, by the 1890s adverts monopolised vehicles, often making it difficult to read the route and destination boards. On many buses, advertisements featured on the inside of stair panels, stair risers, the inside of windows and the underside of the roof as well as on the outside of the vehicle as can be seen here. [1998/75634]

Here a conductor stands on the rear platform that replaced the step at the bottom of the iron ladder. His hand is on a cord that communicates with the driver and along with his enamel licence badge he also carries a bell punch ticket machine. Conductors punched holes in pre-printed tickets with machines like this one made by the Bell Punch & Printing Company. Each fare had a different coloured ticket and by counting the small confetti-like punches collected in the machine at the end of the day, the company could check that the conductor's fare takings were accurate. They were introduced in 1891 and the design, with minor modifications, was used until the 1950s. [1998/84378]

From 1881 horse buses adopted a new design of seat. Known as 'garden seat' buses, they had a number of forward-facing benches on the top deck. Initially introduced by the London Road Car Company, soon all bus firms adopted this design. This early version is an Ealing and Hanwell bus outside Ealing District railway station in around 1885. [1998/86823]

The garden seat was the last major innovation in bus design until the introduction of the motor bus. This LGOC garden seat horse bus is outside the Queen of England public house in Shepherd's Bush in around 1890. The route ran from Starch Green to Bank. [1999/3362]

Here a London Road Car Company (LRCC) garden seat bus is outside
Cedars Yard in West Kensington, August 1894. To the driver's right is a
Union Jack flag on a pole. These were put on all LRCC vehicles in a
patriotic attempt to distinguish the company from the LGOC, which
had French origins. Many people seemed to have forgotten the French
connection so the flag acted more as a route identifier. [1999/6964]

This LGOC bus is outside the Shard Arms on Peckham Park Road. The
driver was a Mr R.J. Reed. [2004/3354]

This LGOC bus was on a route via Monster pub, Pimlico, Westminster Abbey and Bank *c.*1896. [1999/7307]

This vehicle was one of Thomas Tilling's fleet. As mentioned earlier (page 17) Tilling was a jobmaster. He started from humble beginnings owning just one horse. By 1851, just four years later, he had built up enough capital to put his first omnibus on the road. This was the 'Times' and it ran between Peckham and Oxford Circus. He built up his firm until he had over 20 buses, and as well as being a cab owner and liveryman he rented out horses to other firms including tram companies. This 1897 vehicle runs via Wandsworth, Clapham and Battersea. Note the difference to LGOC buses, in that two passengers sit either side of the driver and can share his protective apron. Tilling's buses also carried fewer advertisements. [1998/84905]

This LGOC bus, *c.*1895, is on the Cricklewood to Charing Cross service. [1998/83669]

This LGOC bus on the route between Kilburn and Liverpool Street has stopped outside a Boots chemist shop, *c.*1890. [1998/84678]

Here, an 'Atlas' garden seat bus operated by W.S. Birch and Son can be seen in Trafalgar Square in around 1897, with the National Gallery behind. [1998/84040]

This LGOC bus from around 1900, which ran between Hanwell and Oxford Street, illustrates the popularity of the garden seat design for women. [1998/20639]

This Ealing and Hanwell bus from the early 1900s has room for three passengers next to the driver. It was a feeder service to Ealing Broadway station for the District Railway. [1998/20640]

These two buses are outside the Cannon Brewery in Catford, *c.* 1900. The one on the left is a Thomas Tilling vehicle. Behind the buses is a London County Council (LCC) tramcar. The tram driver holds the Tilling horses' reins at the left of the picture. His brother drives the Tilling bus, his father drives the other vehicle and another brother is the conductor at the right of the picture. [1998/84383]

A number of LGOC garden seat buses wait in line in Edgware Road, *c.*1900.
[1998/55122]

A line of LGOC buses wait in the Strand facing towards the junction with Northumberland
Avenue, Whitehall and Trafalgar Square in around 1900. This picture shows the variety of
different liveries used on the vehicles. [1998/85404]

Here, a driver and conductor here pose with an empty LGOC garden seat bus, *c.* 1900. It seems to have temporary destination slip boards for Loudon Road and Kilburn. [1998/86387]

Here a London Tramways Company garden seat bus is seen with driver and conductor. [1998/55767]

A Finsbury Park to Kent Road LGOC bus, *c*.1900. Today we know the route as 'Old Kent Road'. [2004/3389]

Another LGOC garden seat bus from around 1895 in a posed shot with passengers. The route is from Cricklewood to Charing Cross. [1998/83690]

*Left:* This horse bus is leaving The Gun pub in Pimlico, *c*.1900. [1999/6934]

*Below:* This LGOC bus is on the route from Stoke Newington to Victoria via Islington and Charing Cross, *c*.1902. Again it maintains the 'Favorite' logo of E. & J. Wilson's earlier company. The LGOC bought up many of the smaller horse bus companies to become the largest in London. It reached its peak in 1905 owning 1,418 buses and 17,000 horses. It took a team of six horses to keep one bus running. [1998/82876]

*Above:* This image, taken from a postcard, shows an Atlas and Waterloo Association horse-drawn bus at the Staple Inn, Holborn in 1901. Slightly out of focus, the bus is on the route from Tulse Hill Hotel to King's Cross. [1999/10732]

*Below:* This vehicle is an Edwin Palmer garden seat horse bus. The conductor and an inspector stand beside the bus, which runs from Clapton via Hackney Downs, Liverpool Street and London Bridge to Elephant & Castle. Inspectors were employed when ticketing was introduced to ensure that conductors and drivers kept to time and passed over the right amount of fares. [1998/87093]

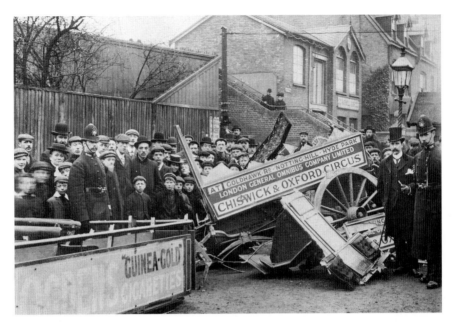

*Above and below:* These two images show the wreckage of an LGOC garden seat horse bus on the Chiswick and Oxford Circus route. The bus was struck by a London South Western Railway (LSWR) locomotive at a level crossing near Grove Park, Chiswick. The top photo shows the separated upper and lower decks of the bus and interior body panels, strewn across the ground. The photograph below shows the mangled lower deck of the bus and interior body panels (displaying Fares board and Pears soap advert). Curious onlookers form a wall of bodies in the background. [1998/83801] & [1998/75118]

A Thomas Tilling bus on the Tooting route is seen in a posed shot with passengers, c.1902 [1998/86825]

This poor quality shot shows a rare photograph of an LGOC experiment between 1902 and 1906. A canvas roof with small transparent windows could be put up in adverse weather conditions. Inside was doubtless gloomy and damp. [1998/56543]

This Tilling bus from 1903 is outside the Raynes Park Hotel. The curtains in the window added a more luxurious feel to the journey. [1999/20209]

The 'Royal Blue' bus company was owned by John Clark and was bought by the LGOC. This photograph of a vehicle maintaining the 'Royal Blue' livery is from around 1909. It has a route number 66. Route numbers were first introduced in November 1908. [1998/56518]

This is one of the last LGOC horse buses. The company built its last horse vehicles in 1905 as motor buses became more popular, although its last horse bus was not withdrawn from service until 1911. London's first petrol-engine bus was put into service in 1899 by the Motor Traction Company and by the end of 1905 there were 241 motor buses on London streets. [1998/55806]

Here two horse buses are seen about to turn a street corner in 1904. The bus to the front is a London Road Car Company (LRCC) vehicle and can be seen sporting the Union Jack. In January 1905 the LRCC announced it was to replace all its horse buses with petrol-engined vehicles. The days of the horse dominating transport were numbered. [1998/20716]

Here three rows of horse buses can be seen at the bus terminus outside the Crown Hotel, Cricklewood Broadway, *c.*1905. A crowd is gathered on the right, around one of the new London Pioneer motor buses. Horse buses had brought visitors to a public trial of the new motor vehicles that would soon replace them. [1998/84541]

This Associated Omnibus Company bus on route 70 is outside Victoria railway station in 1909. Some routes remained horse powered for some years after the motor bus was introduced. Selfridges, seen advertised here, had opened in Oxford Street in 1908. [1999/10737]

*Above and below:* These two Associated Omnibus Company buses are outside Victoria railway station in around 1910. The top 'Royal Blue' vehicle is on route 66 and the one below on route 68. The Associated Omnibus Company was closely linked with the LGOC. [1999/6930] & [1999/10739]

*Right:* This rather atmospheric shot shows a garden seat bus with a passenger in silhouette around 1910. The number of horse-drawn vehicles at this time was dwindling, and the last services would run within the next four years. [1998/13470]

*Below:* This LGOC 'Favorite' horse-drawn bus is on a route between Tollington Park and Victoria via Holloway, Holborn and Westminster in around 1908. At this time the LGOC took over the London Road Car Company (LRCC) and the London Motor Omnibus Company. A year later, in 1909, the LGOC started building its own motor vehicles at Walthamstow. [1998/83700]

This is one of the last City-Atlas horse buses on the London Bridge to Swiss Cottage express route, changing horses outside Swiss Cottage *c.*1910. [1998/86936]

Another of the buses nearing the end of its working life, en route between Clapham Junction and Piccadilly Circus in around 1908. [1998/20674]

*Above and below:* Both of these vehicles are in the LGOC yard, waiting to be sold or broken up. The first is an old knifeboard horse bus and below, a garden seat vehicle. [1998/87203] & [1998/55831]

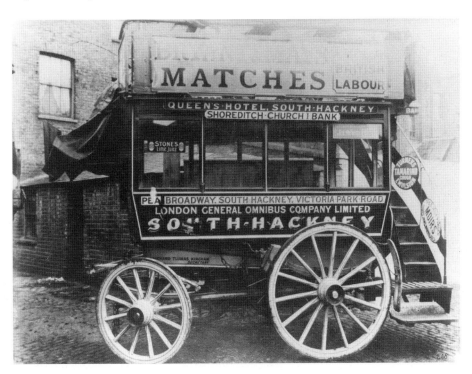

In 1893 W.J. Gordon wrote, 'The London General Omnibus Company are the greatest users of living horse power in London. They have in round numbers, ten thousand horses, working a thousand omnibuses, travelling 20 million miles in a year and carrying one hundred and ten million passengers.' It took many workers to keep the organisation running. This shot of the LGOC North Road coach factory in Islington from around 1900 shows two rows of wooden horse bus bodies supported on frames and the men working on them. [1999/5702]

Not all the vehicles were in use at once and at these times they were at rest or being repaired in the companies' factories. Here the staff who built and repaired the vehicles at the North Road factory pose in front of a bus body frame. [1999/6933]

Perhaps a bigger job than looking after the vehicles was tending the thousands of horses used to pull London's buses. Numbers of animals in one stable varied between 50 for the smaller concerns to 500. Stable hands had to ensure the animals were kept in good conditions. [1999/17400]

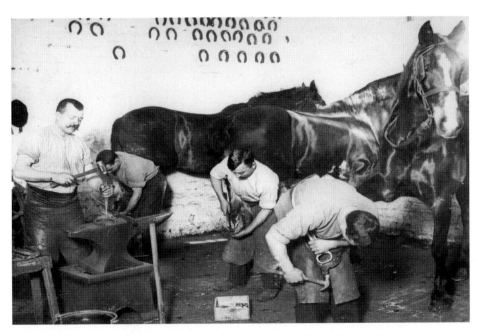

On-site facilities included harness shops, infirmaries and smithies. Blacksmiths, seen here at the LGOC forge, were employed to keep the horses well shod. [1998/86721]

Horses were considered capital goods, an expensive commodity that depreciated in value very quickly. They were the machines that ran the vehicles and as such had to be looked after seven days a week. Each horse had to be fed, watered, groomed and generally cared for, before going on another shift. [1998/55088]

*Right:* Horses got sick whether or not they were working, so on-site infirmaries were essential for stables. This illustration from an 1891 edition of *Black & White* magazine shows a horse in a hospital harness at an LGOC stable.

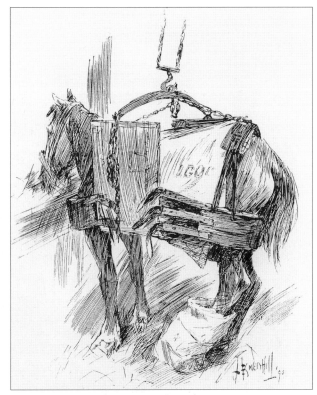

*Below:* This shot of an LGOC horse infirmary in 1911 shows sick horses being looked after. Reports from the 1880s onwards suggest that many stables mistreated their horses in an effort to cut costs. The animals were said to be overworked and were subjected to bad stabling, bad shoeing and had a low standard of conditions. This does not seem to be the case here. [1998/84626]

Stabling horses was expensive. Straw was used for bedding until the 1870s but later this was only for the best horses. Large stable owners experimented with cheaper alternatives such as sawdust and later peat, as can be seen here at an LGOC stable. [1998/86716]

Once purchased some horses were kept until they died or had to be destroyed in order to get the most economic benefit out of them. Others were sold on the second-hand market. LGOC horses tended to last only four and a half to five years in service on average, due to the workload of pulling large heavy vehicles. Here stable hands are leading horses at a two-storey LGOC stable. [1998/86720]

The harnessing of horses and vehicles was a large cost for bus companies, as the equipment did not last long. Here disused harness can be seen hanging in the stable shed in 1911. [1998/86708]

As motor buses took over, more and more routes in London, the horse vehicles disappeared and the stables fell into disuse. Here the empty stalls of one LGOC stable illustrate how things were changing. [1998/86722]

With the passing of the horse bus the animals themselves had no further use for the companies and were either sold or destroyed. Here two horses are being led out of the LGOC stable gates in 1911. [1998/74730]

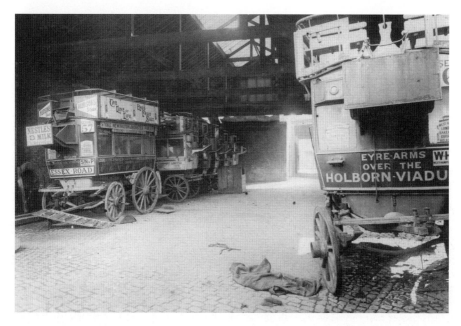

The vehicles themselves were also of no value and fell into disrepair before being destroyed. Here LGOC horse bus bodies wait to be broken up. [1998/86711]

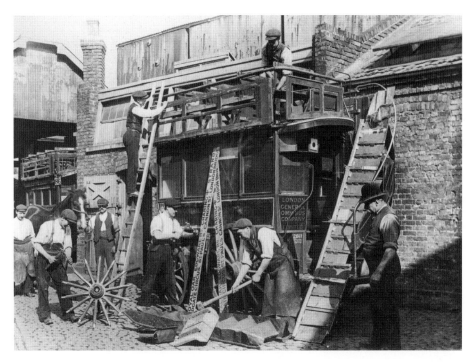

*Above and below:* These two shots show the destruction of the unwanted vehicles in 1911. The only parts worth anything were the wheels that could be sold on. The motor bus was now dominant on most routes although a few horse buses continued to be seen on London's streets until 1914. [1999/3363] & [1998/86710]

*Above and below:* This was the last LGOC garden seat horse bus to operate. It was on service 32 running between London Bridge and Moorgate. The shot above shows the driver and conductor posing on the empty vehicle. The picture below is its last journey as it left London Bridge station full of passengers on 25 October 1911. [1999/6256] & [1999/20636]

*Above:* Some independent operators continued to run vehicles on certain routes although the numbers reduced each year. This image of a bus at Waterloo station was taken in 1913. [1998/55125]

*Below:* In 1914 the last horses were requisitioned by the military for the First World War effort and the horse bus disappeared. This bus, operated by Fred Newman, is probably the last such example to operate on London's streets. [1998/75647]

Very few horse buses survived. This is the only vehicle kept by the LGOC. This photograph, taken at the bus works at Chiswick in October 1926, shows the preserved garden seat horse bus which is still kept today as part London's Transport Museum collection. [1999/9012]

This shot of the LGOC preserved vehicle, again taken in 1926, shows the upper deck and transverse seating for 14 passengers. The driver's seat is separated from the passengers' seats by a metal frame and is complete with a material cover for the legs. [1999/20522]

Some saved vehicles were put to other uses. This garden seat bus dating from 1885 is being deployed as a delivery van for Dolland & Aitchison Ltd in 1944. The opticians used the bus due to imposed petrol rations during the war. The driver was an ex-horse bus driver. Goods were carried on the lower deck of the bus and the conductor allowed people to occupy the top deck of the bus if they were travelling a short way on the route. [1998/55761]

This horse bus of the Star Omnibus Company, seen here in 1943, found new life conveying passengers between Chessington South station and Chessington Zoo. [1998/86937]

Ultimately the wooden horse bus bodies disappeared. Here are the remains of a vehicle found on a Hertfordshire farm in 1957, possibly the last to survive. [1998/74727]

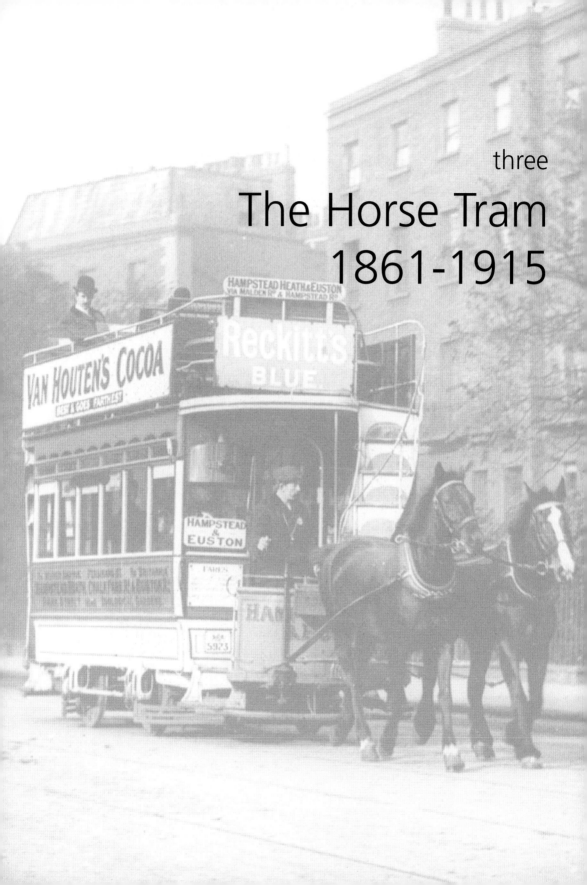

three

# The Horse Tram
# 1861-1915

The horse tram was first introduced by the American George Francis Train, who brought the American-style 'street railways' to London in 1861 after building the first British tramway in Birkenhead in 1860. By this time they were well established in America. Three demonstration lines were laid in London on the Bayswater Road, Victoria Street and from Westminster Bridge to Kennington. Unfortunately the lines were a failure. They used a step rail that protruded from the road and as such caused a nuisance to other vehicles, for which Train was actually prosecuted. The routes of the tramways also typically ran in fairly affluent, carriage-owning areas and as such could not attract passengers. [1998/86353]

THE IMPROVED STREET RAILWAY CARRIAGE.
PATENTED BY GEORGE FRANCIS TRAIN.

This illustration, entitled 'The Improved Street Railway Carriage', depicts two of George Francis Train's horse trams by Marble Arch in 1861. This scene is largely fictitious, as none of the three short lines built by Train actually ran by the Marble Arch, which can be seen in the background. The double-deck tram seen on the right is a complete fantasy.

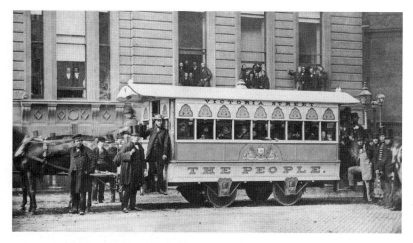

This is 'The People' tram on the second line to be built by Train on Victoria Street. It was a single-deck vehicle and could carry 48 passengers. The line opened on 15 April 1861 and ran between Pimlico station (Victoria station) and the junction of Victoria Street and Tothill Street. Again it used the step rail, which was to prove its downfall. Train was ordered to remove the Bayswater line in October 1861 and the Victoria Street line in March 1862. [1998/56682]

Despite the failure of Train's enterprise, the advantages of the horse tram over the horse bus could clearly be seen. A horse could haul greater loads on rails than over a poorly maintained road, and could carry twice as many passengers as the bus. This meant lower fares could be charged. Attempts to establish trams in London continued and in 1869 a new type of track that was inlaid and therefore flush with the road was introduced. The Metropolitan Street Tramways Company started its first service between Brixton and Kennington in May 1870. This illustration from *The Graphic* magazine shows the interior of this tram.

*Above:* Although the Metropolitan Street Tramways Company was the first to get a route there were two other companies also setting up tramways – the Pimlico, Peckham & Greenwich Street Tramways, and the North Metropolitan Tramways. All three companies had horse-drawn trams and issued cheap workmen's tickets of 1d a mile. Other companies soon followed and the tram quickly became a popular form of transport. This double-deck horse-drawn knifeboard tram, seen here in around 1879, ran from Moorgate Street to Clapton via Hackney Road. [1998/83681]

*Above:* The London Street Tramways Company was set up in 1870 to operate trams in inner north London. It submitted proposals for new lines alongside proposals of the existing three companies, but these met with some opposition. In 1882 the company applied for powers to build a line up Haverstock Hill to Hampstead. Among other objections to the Bill it was stated that, 'Trams will vulgarise Hampstead, and lower its tone as a superior residential suburb'. This highlighted the class difference between horse buses and the horse trams, which were seen more as a working-class form of transport. The Bill was defeated, although in 1886 the company managed to open a line on a parallel street, terminating at Hampstead Heath. This image, from around 1880, is of the staff and head office of the company at 180 Great College Street, Kentish Town. [1998/83646]

*Opposite below:* Special acts of Parliament laid down the regulations for tramways. They were to be built as near as possible to the centre of the road and could not be laid with the nearest rail less than 9ft 6ins from the kerb for a distance of more than 30ft if anyone objected. The width of the rails was to be the standard railway gauge of 4ft 8½ ins and had to be laid level with the surface of the road. This tram, number 226 in the London Tramways Company fleet, was on service between High Street Peckham and St Georges Church via Elephant & Castle in 1879. [1999/20210]

This ticket is issued subject to
the Conditions stated in the
Coy's bye Laws.
All children except infants in
arms to be paid for.
Address all complaints to the
Traffic Manager, 180, Great
College St N. W.

This ticket is issued subject to
the Conditions stated in the
Coy's bye Laws.
All children except infants in
arms to be paid for.
Address all complaints to the
Traffic Manager, 180, Great
College St N. W.

This ticket is issued subject to
the Conditions stated in the
Coy's bye Laws.
All children except infants in
arms to be paid for.
Address all complaints to the
Traffic Manager, 180, Great
College St N. W.

These tickets were issued by
the London Street Tramways
Company in 1875. They featured
bright, colourful advertisements,
which provided an extra source
of income. It is also thought
that they encouraged passengers
to hold on to them so that
conductors would not be tempted
to pick up old tickets and re-issue
them to pocket the fare. They
were not at this time issued with
punches to cancel tickets.

In 1873 two of the original three tramway companies – the Pimlico, Peckham & Greenwich Tramway, and the Metropolitan Street Tramways – joined forces and became The London Tramways Company. This John Stephenson & Co. garden seat tram, seen in around 1882, was run by that company. Stephenson trams were known throughout the world and London's early tram operators imported the vehicles from New York. The London Tramways Company covered a large area of south London, from Waterloo and Southwark to Tooting, Streatham, Camberwell, New Cross and Greenwich. [2003/3540]

The tramways proved highly successful and as early as 1875 LGOC buses were only carrying a few thousand passengers more than the three major tramway companies were. They represented something of a social revolution as they were carrying passengers who had no previous access to public transport. The workmen's tickets opened up a whole new clientele for horse transport. This double-deck knifeboard tram operated between Aldersgate Street and Clapton. It is seen here at Hackney in around 1888. [1998/83680]

This tram, number 244, is seen also operating on the Aldersgate Street to Clapton route, *c*.1888. A panel on the side of the vehicle states that it travels via Hackney Road and the vehicle also displays the licence number 1385. Advertising companies were quick to utilise the vehicles, as they had been on the horse buses, as can be seen from the adverts around the top deck. The conductor in this picture is seen carrying a Bell Punch to cancel tickets. These were introduced in the 1880s, somewhat earlier than on the buses. [1998/83907]

*Opposite above:* This double-deck horse-drawn knifeboard tram, number 261, is on a route between Holborn Town Hall to Stamford Hill via Clerkenwell Road and Kingsland Road in 1888. Passengers can be seen on the upper deck. [1998/83682]

*Opposite below:* Here double-deck tram number 219 is seen in service from Moorgate Street to Clapton, *c*.1888. [1998/87000]

Double-deck tram number 208, en route between Aldersgate and Clapton in 1888. The tram network by this time had reached far out into the suburbs. The City of London and Westminster were closed as far as trams were concerned because the local authority opposed lines being laid within central London. Horse buses still had the monopoly in these areas. [1998/85217]

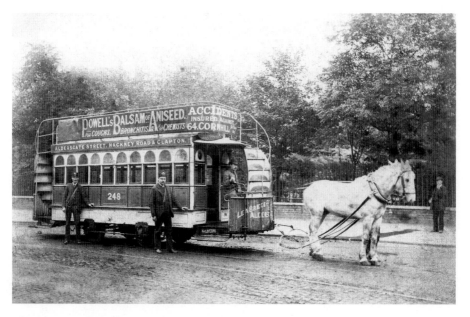

This image is taken from an 1888 postcard. It shows tram number 248 operating between Aldersgate and Clapton and appears to have two conductors. [1998/83703]

A North Metropolitan Tramways (NMT) horse tram, number 148, operating on the route between Moorgate Street and Stamford Hill via Kingsland Road. The tram conductor and driver pose for the camera with other company employees and members of the public in around 1889. By this time there were 14 different tram companies with 130 miles of route carrying in the region of 200 million passengers a year. [1998/75639]

A horse tram outside Clapton Supply Stores, operating on a service between Moorgate Street and Clapton. [1998/44276]

A three-quarter front offside view of London Tramways Company horse tram number 385 on Tooting–Clapham–Blackfriars Bridge route, *c.*1890. The conductor wears badge number 1200. [1998/84042]

A garden seat-type horse tram, number 22, on the London United Tramways Kew–Richmond route, *c.*1900. London United Tramways took over the lines of West Metropolitan Tramways in 1894. There appears to be no advertising on this vehicle. [1998/55982]

This street scene shows a single-horse single-deck tram serving the route via Rotherhithe New Road in 1890. Other horse-drawn traffic can be seen in the road. This was to be the last route for a horse-drawn tram. It ceased in 1915. [1998/44283]

Here the rear of a knifeboard horse tram is seen in City Road at the Angel Islington on a Moorgate to Archway service in 1890. [1998/84195]

A tram pulled by three mules is visible in this late 1890s view looking at the Elephant & Castle. Mules were briefly tried as an experiment but were not successful. An LGOC knifeboard horse bus stands outside the Elephant & Castle public house/hotel and a second horse bus and various horse-drawn carts mingle with pedestrians in the background. [1998/83913]

*Opposite above:* South London Tramways horse-drawn tram number 55, with knifeboard seating, on the service between Wandsworth and Borough in around 1890. Another tram can be seen on the adjacent track. [1998/55995]

*Opposite below:* This shot of a North Metropolitan Tramways garden seat horse tram, number 477, was taken outside Stamford Hill Depot in around 1890. Inspectors, drivers, conductors, foremen and a horse-handler pose with the vehicle. [1998/85059]

Here a London Tramways Company horse-drawn tram is seen at Clapham Common terminus. The dark green knifeboard car, number 163, is a late Stephenson tram with improved stairs. Different colours were used on vehicles to distinguish routes. The vehicle is on a route to Blackfriars Bridge and the photograph was taken from the first floor of the Plough Inn. [1998/20681]

This scene, c.1890, taken from the same place but the opposite side of the road, shows a Stephenson horse tram, number 151, operating between Tooting and Waterloo station, near the Plough Inn. A garden seat horse bus, operating via Camberwell Green and Clapham Common, stands directly outside the Plough. The view clearly shows that horse trams were much larger than horse buses with twice the capacity. [1998/45238]

A double-deck horse tram in traffic on Old Kent Road, on the Greenwich to Blackfriars route, *c.*1890. Both sets of tram tracks are visible. Other horse-drawn vehicles are using the groove of the tram rail to keep a straight path in the street. [1998/84427]

Double-deck horse tram number 15 decorated for Queen Victoria's Diamond Jubilee in 1897. The vehicle is seen here on Brighton Road, Croydon, near the Red Deer public house. [1998/84399]

A London United Tramways tram, on the Uxbridge Road station to Acton service, again decorated in honour of Queen Victoria's Diamond Jubilee in 1897. London United Tramways was formed in 1894 and the managing director, Clifton Robinson, had the vision of electrifying the tram network. The first electric cars ran in 1901. The horse tram's days were numbered. [1998/56632]

Here three trams can be seen amongst staff at Fleet Road Depot, Hampstead. Driver J.J. Hedges stands in the centre of the group. His son also worked for the tramways, eventually retiring in 1946 after 48 years' service. [1998/86719]

Here workmen are laying track for London United Tramways at Hammersmith in 1898. It was very disruptive work and residents often objected. LUT managing director, Clifton Robinson, had the foresight when laying the new track to ensure they would be compatible for the new electric trams that would soon replace the horse vehicles. [1998/20657]

A view of horse tram number 191, on a Tooting to Blackfriars Bridge service. The driver was Charles Bealey and here he poses with the conductor, horse handler and passengers in 1898. [1999/5667]

Double-deck horse tram number 22, at West Norwood terminus on a Brixton to Norwood service in the 1890s. The caption recognises the fact that electrification of the lines would soon end the horse-drawn service. [1998/56645]

Here a driver and conductor pose with tram number 271 at an unidentified depot, *c*.1900. The vehicle runs on a route between Camberwell Green and St Georges Church. The seats on the open top deck are covered with tarpaulins. Other trams can be seen in the background. [1998/55973]

In a similar posed shot, horse tram number 895 is seen with the driver holding the reins in his left hand and the brake handle in his right. He wears the common heavy leather protective apron. The tram is on the Camberwell Green to Vauxhall Bridge route, although the photograph was taken at a depot in around 1900. [1998/55979]

Rear view of a North Metropolitan Tramways double-deck horse tram in Stoke Newington High Street, c.1900. The vehicle is passing the Three Crowns public house on the Stamford Hill and Holborn route. A second horse tram on the same route is approaching from the opposite direction. Two garden seat horse buses can also be seen in the street. [1998/84386]

A North Metropolitan Tramway double-deck horse tram, *c*.1900. The tram, which is on the Hampstead to Moorgate route, was pink with a blue strip on the side panel. [1998/83697]

Here a North Metropolitan Tramways horse tram is pictured together with driver and two horses outside the gates of a North Metropolitan depot in around 1900. [1999/9194]

This postcard view of Dalston Junction station shows a horse tram approaching the camera. A horse bus can be seen further down the road. [1998/44253]

The Archway Tavern at the foot of Highgate Hill was a terminus for both horse buses and trams. [1998/85255]

A North Metropolitan Tramway horse drawn double-deck tram in 1900. [1998/83698]

North Metropolitan Tramway horse tram number 102 with driver and conductor, taken at the corner of Hertford Road, Edmonton, *c*. 1900. [2004/3406]

Here horses and staff can be seen at the large Mare Street stables of the North Metropolitan Tramway, at Hackney in 1901. As with the bus firms, horses were a major capital and revenue expense for the tramways. Companies could clearly see the advantages of electrification, which took off after 1901. [1998/86717]

Portrait of the LCC tramways department head office staff in October 1903, when electrification of lines was well under way. The London County Council replaced the Metropolitan Board of Works in 1889 and in turn took over many tram routes until it was the largest tram system in the country. Agreements with neighbouring systems also allowed cars to travel on each other's lines. In this way the trams provided London with its first integrated mass transport system. [1998/83645]

This group photograph shows London Street Tramways staff at Hampstead Depot in 1903. Two horse-drawn trams can be seen, with the one on the left bearing a destination board for a Hampstead to Angel Islington service. [1998/56619]

Tram staff, ready to depart on a tramway men's outing in 1902 outside the Cock Tavern in Hackney. [1998/83694]

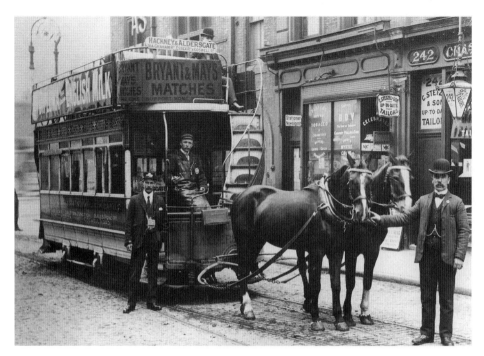

A North Metropolitan Tram Company horse-drawn tram, *c.* 1903. The vehicle is seen outside a shop on the route between Aldersgate and Hackney via Graham Road, Essex Road and Goswell Road. [1998/85260]

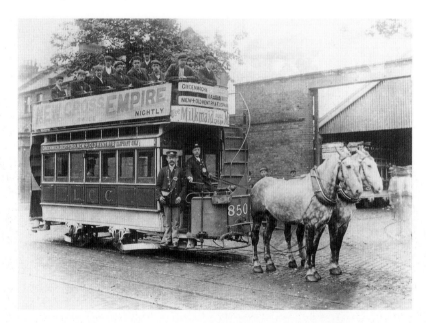

Here LCC double-deck horse tram, number 850, is seen on the Greenwich to Elephant & Castle route via New Cross and Deptford in 1904. The entrance to an unidentified tram depot (possibly Greenwich Road) is visible in the background. The tram driver is George Alfred Darville. [1998/84417]

Here a horse-drawn tram makes light work of the flooded Lea Bridge Road, *c.* 1904. A man in a cart and people in rolled up trousers can also be seen. [1998/20694]

An LCC garden seat horse-drawn tram operates between Hampstead Heath and Euston in 1906. [1998/86863]

These four images are all taken from postcards sold in the early 1900s. This particular card shows a horse tram and other vehicles in The Grove in Stratford in around 1905.

A horse tram and other vehicles are seen here in the street at Clapton Common. This card was posted in August 1905.

This postcard of Camden Road near the Brecknock Arms pub shows two horse buses, a horse tram and a 'growler' cab in the street. It was posted in September 1905.

This horse tram and another horse-drawn vehicle are in the Upper Clapton Road. The postcard was posted in September 1904.

A horse tram and a horse bus in High Street, Camden, in 1905 towards the end of both of their service years. The two vehicles often ran side by side as they attracted different classes of customers and were therefore not seen as competitors. [2004/11814]

This street scene at Bow Bridge in around 1906 shows a horse tram, an electric tram, a motor bus, a cyclist and several pedestrians, highlighting the variety of public transport available to travellers at the beginning of the twentieth century. [2004/12674]

This vehicle was the last horse tram of the Leyton Urban District Council (LUDC), seen here in 1906. It ran on a route to Bakers Arms via Clapton and Markhouse Road. [1998/83642]

This tram, number 17, was the last horse tram on the Harrow Road to Paddington route. The driver and conductor posed to mark the event in 1906. [1998/55273]

The handing over to the new technology can be seen here at Rushey Green, Catford. An LCC electric car, on the left, and an LCC horse-drawn tram, right, are on a Westminster to Catford service. The photograph was taken from the spot where Lewisham Town Hall now stands. [1998/83874]

This shot shows a fleet of electric trams and horse trams at Kennington Park Road. The electrified route opened in May 1903. The horse tram is on the Kennington to Streatham service, which closed for electrification in April 1904. A Class C open-top electric tramcar heads the procession [1998/84329]

This is the London United Tramways (LUT) horse tram on the Kew to Richmond route, seen outside Richmond LUT depot. The image was possibly taken on the occasion of the final run of the tram in 1912. [1999/20407]

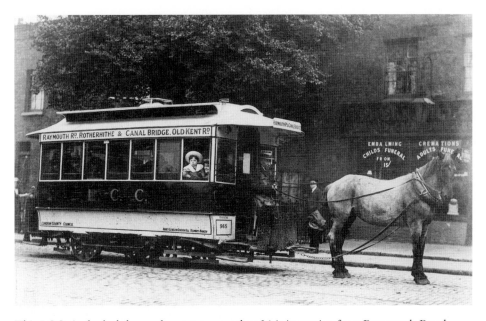

This LCC single deck horse-drawn tram number 36 is in service from Raymouth Road, Rotherhithe to Old Kent Road in July 1913. The tram had a 15ft long body and seated 20 passengers, 10 on each side. It was the very last horse tram and was withdrawn from service on 1 May 1915. [1998/86751]

As with the horse buses before them, horse tram vehicles fell into disrepair or other uses and gave way to the new more modern vehicles, this time electric trams. The remains of this old horse tram, number 41, were being used as a food store for pheasants on a farm in 1905. [1998/89997]

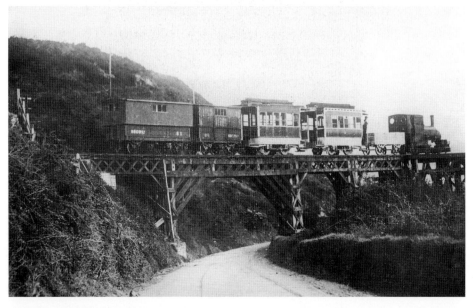

This train hauled by a small steam locomotive on a mineral (china clay) railway in Devon in 1931, used two carriages that were originally North Metropolitan horse tram cars, converted for railway use. [1999/20061]

This old and dilapidated LCC horse tram body was found being used as a garden shed in Molesey, Surrey in 1958. It is a sad reminder of the horse-drawn transport era, which had long since passed. The petrol engine now ran cabs and buses, and electric trams were last used in London in 1952. The horse would never again dominate London's streets. [1998/20612]

# Related titles published by Tempus

## London's Railways

K.A. Scholey

London's Railways gives a unique insight into the history of the railways
in the Capital. This book brings the classic age of rail travel to life and
demonstrates us just how much London was, and still is, dependent on the
shimmering ribbons of steel that have penetrated both over and under the city
from all directions.

0 7524 1605 7

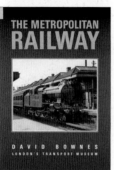

## Metropolitan Railway

David Bownes

The Metropolitan was the world's first underground railway. Opened in 1863,
by 1900 the network reached almost 50 miles into the countryside northwest
of Baker Street and creating suburban 'Metro-land'. This collection of images
charts the Met, which can still boast the furthest destination on the London
Underground today.

0 7524 3105 6

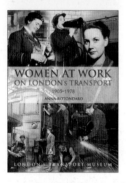

## Women at Work

Anna Rotondaro

The outbreak of the First World War necessitated the development of the then
small female workforce into a major force that would rise to even greater
prevalence in the Second World War, changing the employment sector forever.
This collection of images charts the history of women at work on London's
transport from a typist in 1905 to a tube driver in the mid-1970s.

0 7524 3265 6

## The Willing Servant A History of the Railway Locomotive

David Ross

Taking us through the last two hundred years, David Ross tells not just
the story of the steam engine but also of its effects on mankind. From
small beginnings, the railway locomotive was responsible for the speed of
industrialisation in many countries, for commuting, for tourism, for industrial
progress in all fields and for making the people of the world a transient
workforce. Without it, the world would be a different place.

0 7524 2986 8

If you are interested in purchasing other books published by Tempus, or in case you have difficulty finding any
Tempus books in your local bookshop, you can also place orders directly through our website

**www.tempus-publishing.com**